W9-BMV-262

The FOSSIL FEUD

Marsh and Cope's Bone Wars

O. C. Marsh

E. D. Cope

by Meish Goldish

Consultant: Dr. Luis M. Chiappe, Director
The Dinosaur Institute
Natural History Museum of Los Angeles County

BEARPORT
PUBLISHING

New York, New York

Credits

Cover, © Ken Wagner / PhototakeUSA; Title Page, © The Granger Collection, New York; 4, © Neg. #csgeo4020 / The Field Museum, Chicago; 5, © Neg. #csgeo-4011 / The Field Museum, Chicago; 6, © Louie Psihoyos / Science Faction; 7, © Yale Peabody Museum; 8, © Louie Psihoyos / Science Faction; 9, © The Academy of Natural Sciences, Ewell Sale Stewart Library; 10, © The Academy of Natural Sciences, Ewell Sale Stewart Library; 11, © The Academy of Natural Sciences, Ewell Sale Stewart Library; 12, © William Gallagher; 14, © Yale Peabody Museum; 16, © Yale Peabody Museum; 17, © Yale Peabody Museum; 18, © Francois Gohier / Photo Researchers, Inc.; 19, © Yale Peabody Museum; 20T, © Chris Butler / Photo Researchers, Inc.; 20B, © The Academy of Natural Sciences, Ewell Sale Stewart Library; 21, © Neg# geo85826c, The Field Museum, Chicago; 22, © The Academy of Natural Sciences, Ewell Sale Stewart Library; 23, © The New York Public Library; 24, © Neg. #5519, The American Museum of Natural History; 25, © Louie Psihoyos / Science Faction; 26, © John Eastcott & Yva Momatiuk / Photo Researchers, Inc.; 27, © Louie Psihoyos / Science Faction; 28–29, Rodica Prato; 28, © ticktock Media Ltd.; 29T, Kathrin Ayer; 29B, © ticktock Media Ltd.

Publisher: Kenn Goin; Editorial Director: Adam Siegel; Editorial Development: Natalie Lunis; Creative Director: Spencer Brinker; Photo Researcher: Beaura Kathy Ringrose; Design: Dawn Beard Creative

Special thanks to Eileen C. Mathias at The Academy of Natural Sciences in Philadelphia, and Joyce Gherlone at Yale, Peabody Museum of Natural History

Library of Congress Cataloging-in-Publication Data
Goldish, Meish.
 The fossil feud : Marsh and Cope's bone wars / by Meish Goldish.
     p. cm. — (Fossil hunters)
 Includes bibliographical references and index.
 ISBN-13: 978-1-59716-256-2 (library binding)
 ISBN-10: 1-59716-256-6 (library binding)
 ISBN-13: 978-1-59716-284-5 (pbk.)
 ISBN-10: 1-59716-284-1 (pbk.)
 1. Cope, E. D. (Edward Drinker), 1840-1897—Juvenile literature. 2. Marsh, Othniel Charles, 1831-1899—Juvenile literature. 3. Paleontologists—United States—Biography—Juvenile literature. 4. Paleontology—United States—History—19th century—Juvenile literature. I. Title. II. Series.

 QE22.C56G65 2007
 560.92′273—dc22

                         2006011319

For more information, write to Bearport Publishing Company, Inc., 101 Fifth Avenue, Suite 6R, New York, New York 10003. Printed in the United States of America.

10 9 8 7 6 5 4 3 2 1

Table of Contents

Landslide!

In 1879, a man named W. H. Reed stood at the edge of a cliff in southeastern Wyoming. He looked down at a large **pit** below. In it, two men were digging up dinosaur **fossils**.

In the late 1800s, workers dug up dinosaur bones in pits such as this one in Wyoming.

Reed lifted his pickax. He loosened just enough earth to start a landslide. Huge piles of dirt and rocks tumbled into the pit, burying the men's fossils below.

Reed knew that his actions would please his boss, Marsh. Cope, on the other hand, would be **furious**.

Who was Marsh? Who was Cope? Why were they enemies?

Workers packing up fossils in Wyoming

Some of the world's most famous fossils have come from southeastern Wyoming—especially from a **ridge** called Como Bluff.

Meet O. C. Marsh

Othniel Charles Marsh was an expert on fossils. He was born in New York in 1831. He studied at Yale College in Connecticut and then in Europe.

In 1866, Marsh became a professor of **paleontology** at Yale. At that time, few scientists knew much about fossils. Marsh was the first paleontology professor in North America.

Othniel Charles Marsh

Marsh didn't teach at Yale, however. Instead, he ran the school's new Peabody Museum of Natural History. He eagerly collected fossils for the museum.

Marsh was smart but not very friendly. A neighbor described him as being "always very odd." He never married. People said it was because his only love was fossils.

Many dinosaur fossils can be seen today at the Peabody Museum in New Haven, Connecticut.

Before the 1800s, people knew nothing about dinosaurs. The word *dinosaur* wasn't even invented until 1842.

Meet E. D. Cope

Like Marsh, Edward Drinker Cope was a fossil expert. He was born in Pennsylvania in 1840. As a child he loved to learn about science and nature.

Cope was only 18 years old when he went to work at the Academy of Natural Sciences in Philadelphia. His boss was Dr. Joseph Leidy, the leading fossil expert of his day. Cope helped Leidy organize the Academy's collection of **reptile** skeletons.

Edward
Drinker
Cope

Cope published more than 1,400 scientific papers in his lifetime. That number is still a record today.

Later, Cope studied paleontology in Europe. There he met Marsh. The two men became friends.

Cope liked to work quickly. He was friendly, but he fought with anyone who slowed him down.

The Academy of Natural Sciences, in Philadelphia, is the oldest natural science museum in the United States. It opened in 1812.

Exciting Discoveries

In 1858, Dr. Leidy had received exciting news. A dinosaur skeleton had been dug up in a large **marl** pit in New Jersey. It was the first nearly whole dinosaur skeleton ever found!

Leidy studied the bones. He named the dinosaur *Hadrosaurus*.

Hadrosaurus was a dinosaur with a duck-like bill. Its skeleton drew record-breaking crowds in 1868 when it became the first dinosaur skeleton to be displayed.

Cope believed that more fossils might be found in the New Jersey marl pits. So he began searching there. In 1866, he found the world's second nearly complete dinosaur skeleton. It was named *Dryptosaurus*. Within a year, Cope moved from Philadelphia to New Jersey. It would now be easier for him to hunt for fossils there.

Actual size of a *Dryptosaurus* claw

The word part *-saurus* means "lizard."
Hadrosaurus means "bulky lizard."
Dryptosaurus means "tearing lizard."

The Bone Wars Begin

In 1868, Marsh visited the New Jersey marl pits where dinosaur bones had been discovered. Cope showed his friend around. He introduced Marsh to the workers who had found the bones.

For two weeks, Cope and Marsh hunted for bones. They seemed to work well as a team. Together, they found several interesting fossils.

A marl pit in New Jersey

Fossils have often been found by people digging for something else. Pit workers in New Jersey were digging up marl, which would be used as **fertilizer** to enrich farm soil, when they discovered fossils.

Marsh left New Jersey to return to Yale. Soon, Cope heard news that made him angry. Marsh had snuck back to the marl pits. He had offered money to the pit workers, telling them to send the bones they found to him instead of to Cope. The bone wars had begun!

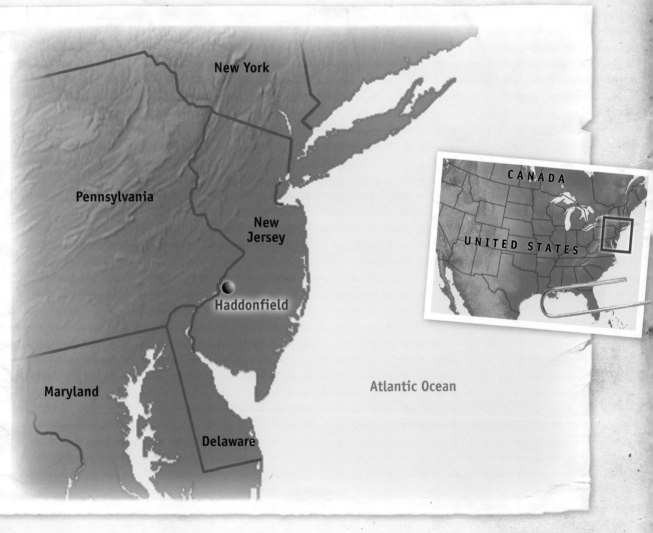

Marsh and Cope searched for fossils around Haddonfield, New Jersey.

The Battle Moves West

The hunt for fossils soon reached other parts of North America. As **pioneers** moved west, they found many dinosaur bones inside rocks and buried under the ground.

In 1870, Marsh hired this group of men to hunt for fossils out west.

Many western pioneers who found dinosaur bones had no idea what they were. One pioneer even built a cabin out of them!

Marsh and Cope traveled west to find fossils for themselves. They were no longer friends, however. They didn't work together anymore. They hired separate work crews to hunt for fossils. These men worked in large areas called **digs**.

Getting bones from a dig was a tough job. Some bones were buried deep in mudstone. Some were stuck in solid rock. Workers used shovels and picks to loosen the chunks of rock that held the bones.

● Digs that produced large numbers of dinosaur fossils

Stealing Fossils

By the late 1870s, crews working for Marsh and Cope were digging up tons of dinosaur bones out west. Each man tried hard to keep the other from getting any bones.

Cope recalled how Marsh had tried to **bribe** workers in New Jersey in order to get fossils. So he decided to try that trick himself.

Marsh's crew of fossil hunters in 1871

Cope snuck into one of Marsh's digs in Wyoming. He secretly hired one of Marsh's workers to bring him fossils.

Marsh was enraged when he found out! So Marsh snuck into a Cope dig and stole some of his fossils. Cope then stole from Marsh. Stealing by both men went on for years.

This 1879 watercolor, painted by one of Marsh's workers, shows fossil hunters with dinosaur bones in Como Bluff, Wyoming.

Over the years, Cope collected thousands of dinosaur fossils. He needed two large houses just to store them all!

Spying and Destroying

Marsh and Cope each used spies. A spy would enter an enemy dig. He might pretend to be selling groceries. He was really there to steal.

Once, Cope himself spied on a Marsh dig. Later, he published an article on what he had seen. He made it sound like *he*—not Marsh—had found the bones!

More than 250 boxes of fossils were shipped to Marsh from this quarry in Canon City, Colorado.

Cope and his workers sometimes used code words when sending messages about fossils and digs. The code words prevented Marsh from getting hold of the information.

Cope and Marsh hired spies to destroy each other's fossils, too. A spy would sneak into an enemy dig and use **dynamite** to blow it up. Sometimes, crews even blew up their own dig after their work was done. They didn't want the enemy to find any more bones there.

Marsh (back row, center) holds a hammer for digging fossils out west. His crew carries rifles in case of an attack.

Huge Mistakes

Throughout their **careers**, Marsh and Cope both hurried to put skeletons of **prehistoric** animals together. Each man wanted to be the first to discover and name new **species**.

The big rush led to mistakes, however. Cope put together a sea reptile called *Elasmosaurus* with the head at the wrong end. Marsh told everyone about the error.

Elasmosaurus was the giraffe of sea reptiles. Its long neck had 72 bones.

Yet Marsh made mistakes, too. Once, he built a new dinosaur skeleton and named the species *Apatosaurus*. Later, he built another skeleton and labeled it *Brontosaurus*. Scientists later found that both creatures were really the same species.

Marsh even built his *Brontosaurus* incorrectly. It had the head of a *Camarasaurus*!

This photo shows a correct skeleton of *Brontosaurus*. Its true scientific name is *Apatosaurus*.

Marsh's *Brontosaurus* wore the wrong head for about 100 years. His mistake was not corrected until 1981.

A drawing of an *Elasmosaurus* skeleton

Telling the Newspapers

By 1890, the war between Marsh and Cope had grown much worse. Finally, Cope could take no more. He complained to the *New York Herald* newspaper. He accused Marsh of taking credit for the work of other scientists. He called Marsh's own work a "remarkable collection of errors and ignorance."

Dr. Joseph Leidy grew very upset by the fighting between Marsh and Cope. He quit paleontology and took up other areas of science instead.

Dr. Joseph Leidy

The next week, Marsh spoke out in the same newspaper. He called Cope his "bitter enemy." He said he even had "some doubts as to his **sanity**."

The newspaper printed stories on the bone wars for two weeks. Many scientists were embarrassed. They felt Marsh and Cope had given paleontology a bad name.

On January 12, 1890, the *New York Herald* made the bone wars public. News of the bone wars sold many newspapers, but it upset many scientists.

PROFESSOR COPE.

PROFESSOR MARSH.

NEW YORK HERALD, SUNDAY, JANUARY 12, 1890.—OCTUPLE SHEET.

SCIENTISTS WAGE BITTER WARFARE.

Prof. Cope, of the University of Pennsylvania, Brings Serious Charges Against Director Powell and Prof. Marsh, of the Geological Survey.

CORROBORATION IN PLENTY.

23

The Bone Wars End

Stories about the bone wars hurt Marsh's and Cope's careers. The U.S. government grew unhappy with both men. Congress had **funded** much of their work. Now members of Congress felt it was a waste of money. They cut off support for new fossil research. Marsh and Cope found it hard to continue.

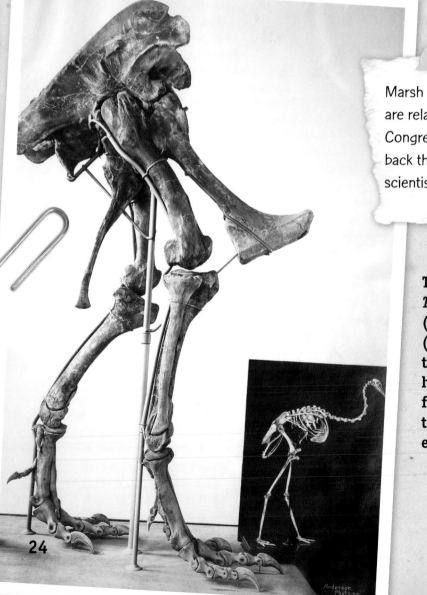

Marsh believed that birds are related to dinosaurs. Congress laughed at the idea back then. Yet today, many scientists agree with Marsh.

The skeletons of *Tyrannosaurus rex* (left) and a bird (right) show that the two animals have many similar features—such as three main toes on each foot.

24

Both men soon went broke. Cope had to sell part of his fossil collection. Marsh had to borrow money to keep his house.

In 1897, Cope became ill. He died on a cot, surrounded by piles of bones. Marsh, a sad, bitter man, died in 1899. After nearly 30 years, the bone wars were finally over.

Cope donated his body to the study of science. Scientists studied his brain and skull after his death.

Good Comes from Bad

The bone wars had surely been harmful. Yet the **feud** also helped science in many ways. Before 1850, only about a dozen dinosaur species were known in North America. Together, Marsh and Cope found over 140 new species. Their discoveries sparked a new interest in dinosaurs around the world.

Marshosaurus, **named after its discoverer**

Marsh and Cope each had dinosaur species named for them. *Othnielia* and *Marshosaurus* were named for Marsh. The species *Drinker* was named for Cope.

Tons of dinosaur fossils were dug up during the bone wars. Today, many science museums in America have at least one skeleton of a dinosaur named by Marsh or Cope.

Many of the two men's fossils aren't even on **display** yet. They're still stored in boxes. Scientists haven't had enough time to study them all!

CERATOSAURUS NASICORNIS, Marsh. ¼

This photograph shows objects from the lives of Marsh and Cope, including Marsh's pick, a *Dryptosaurus* claw, photos of the fossil hunters, and Cope's skull.

A Trip Back in Time:
Marsh's and Cope's Dinosaurs

Marsh and Cope fought a lot with each other. However, they also helped the field of paleontology. Marsh identified 86 new species of dinosaurs. Cope identified 56 new species. Here are three of their most famous discoveries.

Allosaurus

Named by Marsh, this large meat-eater was one of the most powerful hunters in the western United States.

FACTS

Allosaurus
(al-oh-SOR-uhss)

- name means "strange lizard"
- lived 150 million years ago, during a time scientists call the late Jurassic period
- had 3 razor-sharp claws, each 4 inches (10 cm) long, on each hand
- **size:** about 20 feet (6 m) long

Camarasaurus

Named by Cope, this plant-eater probably roamed in large groups.

FACTS

Camarasaurus
(*kam-uh-ruh-SOR-uhss*)

- name means "chambered lizard"
- lived at the same time as *Allosaurus*
- walked on four large legs, all about the same size
- stripped leaves off trees
- **size:** about 75 feet (23 m) long

Stegosaurus

Named by Marsh, this plant-eater stood out because of the two rows of bony plates that ran along its back. The largest of these plates could have reached 2 feet (.6 m) tall.

FACTS

Stegosaurus
(*steg-uh-SOR-uhss*)

- name means "roofed lizard"
- also lived at the same time as *Allosaurus*
- had a small head with a brain the size of a golf ball
- had long spikes on its tail, which it swung to keep enemies away
- kept its head close to the ground for eating low plants and fruits
- **size:** about 15 feet (4.5 m) long

Glossary

bribe (BRIBE)
to offer money or a gift to get someone to do something that is usually wrong

careers (kuh-RIHRZ)
work done by people, usually for a long period of time

digs (DIGZ)
places where people dig for the ancient remains of plants or animals

display (diss-PLAY)
a public show

dynamite (DYE-nuh-mite)
a very powerful explosive used to blow up something

fertilizer (FUR-tuh-*lize*-ur)
a substance added to soil to make plants grow better

feud (FYOOD)
a bitter argument between two people or groups that lasts for a long time

fossils (FOSS-uhlz)
what is left of plants or animals that lived long ago

funded (FUHND-id)
gave money to pay for something

furious (FYU-ree-uhss)
angry

marl (MARL)
a rich, clay-like substance

paleontology (*pale*-ee-uhn-TOL-uh-jee)
the study of ancient plants, animals, and rocks

pioneers (*pye*-uh-NEERZ)
people who go to live in a place that is not yet settled

pit (PIT)
a wide, deep hole that has been made in the ground

prehistoric (*pree*-hi-STOR-ik)
more than 5,500 years ago, which was before the time when people began to use writing to record history

reptile (REP-tile)
a cold-blooded animal that usually has dry, scaly skin, such as a lizard, snake, turtle, or crocodile

ridge (RIJ)
a narrow chain of hills or mountains

sanity (SAN-uh-tee)
having a healthy mind

species (SPEE-sheez)
groups that animals are divided into, according to similar characteristics; members of the same species can have offspring together

Bibliography

The Academy of Natural Sciences. "Bone Wars: The Marsh-Cope Rivalry."
www.acnatsci.org/museum/leidy/paleo/bone_wars.html (2005).

Dobson, G. B. "The Bone Wars: From Wyoming Tales and Trails."
www.wyomingtalesandtrails.com/bonewars2.html.

Hellman, Hal. *Great Feuds in Science: Ten of the Liveliest Disputes Ever.* New York:
John Wiley & Sons (1998).

Huntington, Tom. "The Great Fossil Feud in the American West" from *American
History* magazine (August 1998). **www.historynet.com/ah/blgreatfeud/index.html**.

Levins, Hoag. "Haddonfield and the 'Bone Wars.'" **www.levins.com/bwars.shtml**.

Read More

Dixon, Dougal. *The Search for Dinosaurs.* London: Thomson Learning (1995).

Goldish, Meish. *Fossil Tales.* Philadelphia, PA: Chelsea Clubhouse (2003).

Green, Tamara. *Great Dinosaur Hunters.* Milwaukee, WI: Gareth Stevens Publishing
(1999).

Hartzog, Brooke. *The Dinosaur Bone Battle Between O.C. Marsh and Edward Drinker
Cope.* New York: PowerKids Press (1999).

McMullan, Kate. *Dinosaur Hunters.* New York: Random House (1989).

Learn More Online

Visit these Web sites to learn more about the discoveries of Marsh and Cope:

www.factmonster.com/ce6/people/A0813461.html

www.strangescience.net/cope.htm

www.strangescience.net/marsh.htm

Index

About the Author

Meish Goldish has written more than 100 books for children. His book *Fossil Tales* won the Learning Magazine Teachers' Choice Award.